My first experience of M:
work was in the autumn
the Gorsedd of the Bards. As I watched him
perform his rhymes I became delighted. Mark
has a fresh take on the craft of a bard, and his
energy is a joy to behold. As I listened to his
wonderful words, his rhymes within lines, his
consonance, assonance, alliteration and delicate
phrases, as I watched him walk his rolling
rhythms round the ring, I knew I was seeing
something special.

This is the first book of the Dragon Fly, and it is in
the reading of it that I have truly come to know
and love his work.

In this book you are invited to walk the circle of
the year with him, to rejoice in the sacred beauty
of the Earth with him, to sense the subtleties of
the seasons, of sunshine and of shadow with him,
to see how the muse moves within him, and to
share in his wildest and wittiest imaginings.

How freely the forces of life flow through him on
to the page! What pictures he paints with his
words! Come, come, dance with the Dragon Fly!

Here is a magical thing. Here is a book full of
wisdom and light. Here is an innocent, beautiful
thing. Here is a glimpse of a true poet's soul.

Mark the Bard

There once was a Druid called Mark
Who could slam about Sun and the spark
Whilst not whiter than white
He was less of the night
And more of the day than the dark

A Bard from the Avebury hood
He would whittle his words from the wood
Add a berry of yew
And some mistletoe, too
And bang in the net...he was good

My Goddess, that Druid could rap
In the spring he could draw up the sap
And in winter could beat
Up the heat through his feet
Pretty neat...give the Druid a clap

Gail Foster

Contents

Cover art by Vikki Yeates
Editing and interior by Gail Foster

Dragon Fly Poetry

ISBN-13:
978-1721251520

ISBN-10:
1721251529

Dragon Fly Poetry

>¦<

Mark Westmore

This book is dedicated to
my Friends and Family
and all the marvellous people
I have met on this
Magical Journey
through
Life

Ode To The Dragonfly

Wake from liquid slumber
Aqua skating hunters
Bloom from neon waves
Shimmering light lions
Roaring sky orchids
Soaring swarms form
Delicate storms of blossom
Then gently fall
Back to their pool
Never to be forgotten

>¦<

Forgotten Lines

Here's a nod
To all the lines we've forgotten
All the words lost like starved paths
Our wandering hearts have left untrodden

We may not remember the details
But our souls are still awash with feeling
In between now and forever
Like a thousand embers, on the wind
Still gleaming

My Skin Is Ink

My skin is ink
I shed words and share hairs
Brush strokes flair
Fizzing embers fired from a thoughtful mind
Words cast upon burning wings
I bare to you my bones

My blood is ink
I bleed for free
Sunken treasures gush from crimson
Passion found in rhyme and rhythm
Words cast upon burning wings
Spiralling...

Into the unknown

The Life Force

Unforgotten Embers

The seeds were planted
Long before you even began to remember
The rising Dragon belongs to songs and stories
Still burning strong from unforgotten embers

Gloriousness

O gloriousness that bore us
And set us on our way
Through stardust
Then through the Milky Way
It fired us;
Enormous
Distances we made
Advances
Then atoms joined again
The chances
Were less than anything
Disasters
Couldn't kill the string
Then faster
Life began to spring
Like mountains
Creating everything
We're fountains
Flourishing we bring
The answers
The cosmos is our king
Enhance us

The Source

Stand tall
Let your roots
Fall and form

Plug into the force
From which you were born

Connect to the source
From where all is drawn

Electric Nectar

We are light beings
Charged by the Sun
A million white flowers
Blooming through our bloodstream

Harvesting electric nectar
Feeling energy pulse inside our veins

We siphon the fire and dance with the flames

Cosmic Awakening

Everything is alive
Eternity etched across the Sky
The light of a million eyes
Inside our head, and our hands
Energy in every strand

A cosmos within us
Art in grains of sand and stars
Each start the same
Life's flame is ours

In all who come
Are hearts of Sun

We are but one
We are but one

Before All This

Before all this
Beneath an unscarred sky
Beyond distracted minds
In times gone by

Around a fire pit
Where stories stray
And red flames lick
The end of days

Back From Where We Came

Back from where we came
To the stars that started it all
Carved from worlds of flame
Sculpted by firefalls

Our journeys are the same
We can see our mothers call
Back from where we came
Their light still touches all

Sands Of Time

I see
All of the kisses that have poured into the making
Of me

A thousand loves lost to the sands of time
Glorious, laborious stories
Of coincidence and connection

When my eyes meet myself in a mirror
A million shards of glass sculpting my reflection
I realize, that history was on my side

Those who have rode into the night
Left me a body

Those who have fallen
Gave me life

Harness Your Power

There are no certainties
During this cosmic journey
Nothing is known for sure

Yet, if we stare but for a minute
Into the complex abstract
Over worlds of stars
Stretching further
Than we can even begin to imagine

We realise that there is more than enough
Room to dream
More than enough space to fathom
That our actions matter
And our power can be mightier than
Comprehension itself

Free

And we were free
From form and all of thought
In the moment nothing mattered
Free from definition
All the labels they had scattered
Because all we are
All we've ever been
Is the same connected web
From dark to light
And light to dark
The soul is never dead

A Force Living Wildly

ENERGY keeps flowing
It's growing
And going much faster
The master of all things

It's speeding and coursing
Life is performing
It's talking and courting
And chortling inside me

A force living wildly

We Are Here

We're a spark from the infinite
Intimately intricate
Animated elemental
Collaborating with potential
Articulating existential
We are here! That's pretty mental

Light Beings

Spectacular, vernacular synergy
We are human beams
Of omnipresent imagery

Light beings with feelings
The Universe is ours
We are ever present energy
The sparkle in the stars

Universe

I give respect to the Universe
From whence I came
I give respect to a force
That needs no name
Creation itself
Need not be explained
Beginnings and endings
Are one of the same

Thanks

I give thanks to the Life Force
To the Great Spirit that flows
Through all things

The
Rhythm

The Rhythm

We come from the rhythm of the Sea
We come from the rhythm of the Sea
We come from the rhythm of the Sea

We come from the wet depths, feel air surge
Through the gaps in your treasured chest
Creatures aren't ready, features aren't present yet
The Sea will be revealed through tears and sweat

Sweet – fresh – first – breath
We – rise –from – the – depths

Crawling on our bellies, hauling up the shores
Tentacles flaying, bodies baking
Being raked by the beach's sandy claws

Once again we pause for breath...

Hear waves beat
Like the hearts in your treasured chest

Red roots splayed, bottom rung on the spine >

27

All must rely on the passage of time
From grounding comes growth
Survival is key
Ruby runes are entombed by the Sea's energy

Pounding waves – rhythmic swathes
Of booming tunes – from the first Full Moon

Born through sex and pleasures bright
Sacral horns pipe off delight
Orange glows from wombs descend
A flaming brook connects two ends
Born from fire, offspring is spewed
Liquid rhyme collects-colludes
Charging forward we have just begun
We come from the rhythm
We come from the rhythm

We come from the rhythm of the Sun

Amber clad flotilla sails
Light lugger ship fins and lizard skin tails
In oozing swamps where steam collects
Protruding reptile scales reflect

Solar beams of bright Yellow light
The plexus seems to draw strings tight
Synapses will unite and swell
Let life drink from the neuro well
Like bubbles intelligence has risen
We come from the
We come from the

RHYTHM

Stagnant pools squirt out warm blood
New creatures crawl from the clay and mud
Juddering jets begin to calm
And smoothly split like veins through arms
Splashing, crashing, rushing streams
Turn parched pastures to a stunning Green
Inner ink crafts unique design, pulsing, pulsing
Inner ink crafts unique design
Pulsing hearts from the divine

We come from the rhythm of space and time

Hollering fast paced high pitch cries
Stunning plumes swoop across lazuli Blue skies >

Near lakes where troops of primates gather
Hear echoes from throats that whoop and jabber
By the shore where water meets land
Patterns are scraped and scrawled by hand

Creative shapes, ideas expand
A new dawn beckons for the age of man
Trapped inside this conscious prison
We are the rhythm
We are the rhythm
Use the gifts we have been given

WE ARE THE RHYTHM

Knowledge spirals through Indigo eyes
Yet raging rivers of anger rise
Torrents of tolerance start to fade
When Jupiter sized egos invade
Kneeling before digital currents
Pineal glands become redundant
We must dream to sail up stream
We must dream, we must dream

Shift perceptions in changing times

We are the rhythm
We are the rhythm
Shift perceptions in changing times
We are the rhythm

WE ARE THE RHYME

Our deepest wish is to transcend
But first this global ship must mend
Plug leaks with love, let's not be stern
For there is so much more to learn
Wear our Violet crowns with pride
Gently be taken by the tide

We have flowed through history
Go back to the rhythm
Back to the rhythm
We have flowed through history, go
Back to the rhythm of the Sea

The Moon

The Moon Grove

Trickling roots from the beech tree
Point me towards the Moon grove
Where sunken stones absorb echoes
From those who chose to follow the patterns of
Our globe

Black Moon

Black Moon of new beginnings
Please heed to grant a wish

Bring a freshness
To our senses
During this
Lunar genesis

Lunar Light

Living and learning by lunar light
Patterns keep turning
Passions keep burning
Magick is working
As long as I'm serving
The Moon as it moves
Through the night

New Moon Nomad

New Moon nomad
Nocturnal stroller
Owls hoot as I stoop
In my boots
Scooting along
Through gloopy soil
Enrolled in the night's meditation

Patterns In The Shadows

In the patterns of the shadows
Where our fair lady hides
A new tide is turning
A new phase begins to rise

Washed By Time

As the last embers of daylight die
Above the trembling Corsican sky
A New Moon, worn just like a shell
Washed by time as she rose and fell

Pulled By The Strings

Sailing the streams
Doing my thing
Pulled by the strings
Of the Moon
As it sings

Waxing

The Moon is waxing
I see a smile rising
A hook prising
A claw to draw me in
A pin curving
A grin swerving
Light branded on its skin

Tell Us A Tale

The night is still
The air is warm
Pale shadows spill
Across the lawn

Swarming thoughts
Now gently quell
As minds are soothed
By a silver spell

Tell us a tale
With a blissful end
Tell us a tale
To help us mend

Lost In Her Glow

It's easy to get lost in the Moon
There's a part of us in there
Somewhere

Our glances caught by her glow

Stories told below
Her pale white light
Still echo across space and time

Her phases are the silent chimes
The silver lines on the pages of our lives

Moon Shepherds

Flocks of cloud are parting
As daylight turns to dark
But the people are departing
Instead of following the heart

Too many of us bleating
Steeped in a sheepish white
The wolves will keep on eating
Until we put things right

We are shepherds of the people
Show them love's the only way
The Moon's in us, we can win this
Don't become their prey

Womb Of The Moon

The womb of the Moon
Still lurks
In the way that
The Earth works

Without her impact
There wouldn't be this
A precision collision
A stormy kiss

Moon Rose

The Moon rose
To spread its silver toes
And those limbs of pale grey light
Go creeping through the night

Looming Moon

The Full Moon's looming
It's time to tune into
Some super human
Communion

Outpost

Outpost of the night
Ghost of the Sky
Hosting the dark
With a pearly white eye

Rituals

A Moon for our rituals
And the falling of walls
Shrines shine
With candles
And magical tools

Intentions are vented
To enter her pull
And illuminate sigils
Drawn by our calls

Scrying below
A ballooned crystal ball

Go Outside

Go outside, she calls you there
Go outside, to meet her stare
Feel her pull
Through the cool night air
Go outside, she wants you there

Her body's bare
Wearing scars with pride
She's full of magic...

Go outside

Moonlight Talks

Moonlight talks in silver tongues
Breathing in secrets through rocky lungs

Tides Of Bliss

Tides of bliss are tied to this
You'll never tire of this
Love is forever
Move with the Moon
She'll bring us together

Moon Charmer

I saw the Full Moon this morning
With a draping, grayish, cloudy awning
A ripe light gem, plump for fawning
So I talked her down as a storm was spawning

She got in my car saying "Thank you darling
That cold winter air is quite alarming
And as for you, you're very charming"
I said "thank you ma'am." My words were calming

Now, Mrs Moon started yawning
She'd been up all night and the day was dawning
So she fell asleep and I went pawning
Swapped the Moon for the Sun this morning

Sequential Spell

The Full Moon
Is always shared
Wherever we are on this planet

A magnet of magnificence

Senses sharpened
With hearts enlarged
Let us march towards
Our full potential

The magick of invention
And reinvention swells
Lunar blasts cast
By a sequential spell

Charge Your Intentions With Power

By the light of the Full Moon
Charge your intentions
With power

The Written Word

Words Inside

The poets weren't buried with words inside

They gave us a gift

That cannot die

Each verse and quote

Is rooted deep

They gave us a gift

That will always speak

Yet To Dream

I'm in love with the poems
I haven't written
And the places I've never been
The people I've never met
And the dreams left
Yet to dream

Warm The World

My time is worth burning
When words can warm the world

My time is worth burning
To break out of this shell
Use the fire to propel
Snap the chains
And break the spell

Sky Canvas

Today my mind's like shifting clouds
Never settling on a theme
I wish for words to fall like rain
To tell you what I've seen
I saw a picture in the Sky
That stole my thoughts tonight
A spire of white in front of grey
Lit by a golden light
I can't explain the revelry
Or the grandeur of this scene
But leave you with some imagery
To grasp at what I mean

Nature Is My Paper

Nature is my paper
The gold within my quill
The healer of my racing mind
Her presence keeps me still

And in the calmness
Of her clutches
When all I do is feel
Everything comes naturally
The words begin to spill

Storer Of Stories

No rest for the poet, no rest indeed
Said the man as he pulled a pen from his sleeve
Covered in leaves he started to write
Exploring the floor as the day became night
Riddles and symbols leapt from his hand
Wriggled with rhythm, began to expand
He started to weave an intricate web
Soothsaying flavours sprung from his head
You see a pen can be magic, a modern day wand
A storer of stories, soaring beyond

The Poet

I think in poetry
Showered by words constantly
A rhythmic rattling in the brain

Untamed tangents spin off handily
Rowdy clouds form complex imagery
Falling deeply, randomly and continuously
Between each drop of thick, thinking, inky rain

It's like some kind of strange geometry

Minds strains and pen pains
Are just part of the game
And within the watery pits of passion
I'll continue to make it happen
Happily letting it kill me
Even if it's without a penny to my name

Curious Minds

I'm bored with keyboards
And types of type
And endless tappings
Below screens of light

I request

Flickering candles
And midnight quills
With inky whirlpools
That gentle spill
Enthralling stories
From bygone times
That open doorways
To curious minds

Interject

So many poems we have inside
Have not been invented yet
As words tumble from a
Conjuring mind
To spill and interject

.

Muster The Muse

Grazing at the gates of eternity
Gazing within the sublime
Confines of our time
I confide with my maker
The Universe

We are ourselves creators
From dust we can muster the muse

Amuse ourselves, confuse ourselves
Dither and wither, but we will deliver
It's in our nature
To put pen to paper
To scrawl

Let words fall like shooting stars
Let thoughts tumble from the
Jumbled jungle that is the mind

Let's roar

Sounds ripple across fragile skies
Scattering sonic waves

This is our time
We are alive
Let's make the most of it

Have A Spin

Wonderful words
Glistening like silk
Are built to pull
Us in
So
Build more bridges
Weave less walls

Be sure to have
A spin

Senses

I like the notion
Of playing around with senses
Why separate the fields
When you can rip down the fences
Why pick and choose, instead infuse
Use them where they're not intended

Inspirations

Who Crows There

Who crows there
In the silver veil
Of fog that feeds
The night?

Make Things Happen

Grow in grace
Embrace the challenge
Face each storm, head on
And make things happen

Flames

Untame your flames!
Lay claim to your passion
Let your soul glow
In the fires of action

Peace

Make peace
With all our pieces
Realise relief
And what it releases

Sum Of Our Thoughts

We are what we think
Every choice, every start
So let go and follow
What you hold in your heart

Frozen Wings

Frozen wings are beating
Heating fire in my soul
I know that time is fleeting
As I fly towards my goal

Sprawled Wings

In the Sky we find feeling
Sensation and healing
The ceiling to all things
Supporting our sprawled wings

Choose The Path

As the Sun is about to break
Make a vow in the vermilion wake
To choose the path
You were born to take

Wishes

The best poems and people
Seem to fall upon us like
Shooting stars
Our wishes were never wasted

Feel With Every Breath

For those who are born with a mermaid soul
Will never fear the depths
With hearts the size of oceans
They feel with every breath

True Beauty Emerges

In this crazy world around us
Beyond this modern moulded circus
If we look below the surface
True beauty emerges

You Can

You can
If it is chosen
A plan can melt the frozen
A hand can lead the broken

Lion Heart

Live life with a lion heart
Courage is contagious
Taking action when you're afraid
Can lead to positive changes

The Future

The future's exciting
Open, inviting
Nothing's in writing
The prospect's enticing

The Caterpillar

I promised to the caterpillar
That I would stretch my mind
And believe that I could find
The strength to help me fly

Multicoloured Lives

In the madness and the melee
Of our multicoloured lives
Lives the stillness and the realness
From where we are derived

Stoned Blessings

Write your worries in the sand
Let the winds of time be blown
Then with a thankful hand
Carve your blessings into stone

Sipping Bliss

Have a quick sip from your dreams
Let's taste a wish
Because our souls are full of flavours
And our minds are full of bliss

Behind The Art

No one will ever slay the Dragon
That's living in my heart
The Dragon is the passion
That lives behind the art

Train The Brain

Train the brain to stay on track
Always forward, never back
What is taut, shall never slack
We can gain what we lack

Unforgotten Poems

Kind words blossom
Into unforgotten poems
Dispersing seeds of joy
That will continue growing

Fractals Of Lovely

Sipping in the scenery
From the flower
That governs me
Overlapping fractals of lovely

Damsel Dance

Damsels dance
In summer's haze
Reflecting light
In powerful ways

Field Of Stars

I walk below a field of stars
Below a million suns that shine
And know that in some way we are
Part of the same design

Sky Dragons

Sky Dragons have awoken!
Woven wings now hum
Floating around a golden shore
Glistening in the Sun

Spin Drift

Days like waves
Go rushing by
As our lives cascade
Through spindrift skies

Warm Bolt

Struck by a warm bolt
Lured to her cult
Through no fault of my own
Now I'm never alone

Enter

Every doorway
Has a story
Enter, to find your centre
Enter, and open your mind

Make A Wish

Make a wish my darling
Because the stars, they fall for you
Then just like me, maybe you'll see
The wish you made come true

Fly

If you want to fly
Don't let doubt weigh you down
You are vast and brilliant
Strong, resilient
Go craft your own crown

Crestfallen

The One

Another day has passed me by
My heart sinks like the Sun
For I have gazed upon a hundred flowers
Yet still can't pick the one

Enough Time

I've had enough time
To see how I've grown

I've got enough time
To change what I've blown

Bring Me Back

There is a path I need to take
But from the past I must escape

Depart from old bones, ways and woes
That keep me buried
In the ground below

Let the light in

Let me speak

Bring me back
From silent sleep

Aftermath

I'm caught up in the aftermath
Of moments as they pass
Resisting work for pleasure
Trying to walk the easy path

Won't be the hardest worker
To only finish last
Resistance, she is lurking
I just want to have a laugh

I'm caught up in the aftermath
Of moments as they pass
Pushing things to next week
My writing time is sparse
And the days they spiral past
On a ship without a mast

This time I'm taking action
To break the spell that's cast
Don't want a life of sorrow
Because I didn't have the heart
Because I never made a start

Evasive

I'm trying to find my peace
Trying to find my place
In a world of faces
But it's so evasive

Words tumble from the sheets
But my day's stuck on repeat
I need to find new places
And get back to basics

Escape

Sometimes we can't escape the shapes

That break across our gaze

Stranded by inaction we just watch away the days

In a melancholy maze

But this storm is just a phase

Soon we'll be able to find our

Way across the waves

Dancing For The Lost

The night carries a rhythm
That the day left off...

Dancing for the lost

Shrunken Suns

The pale stars are rising

Pathways appear over the horizon
Guiding us towards part of ourselves
We've lost to the dark

Past the places we care to remember
Past the pits of despair and endeavour
On stilts, tired eyes slit
Rain comes in fizzes and spits
As we melt like shrunken suns

Try

At the least we try
To write songs in our hearts
To play but a part
In this sonnet

And with it we lay
Our time
& our days
Our life
& our ways
Fly from it

Peace Of Mind

RELEASE
Let it go
It may be slow
It may be heavy
Usually we're holding on
When the cargo's gone already

We cannot trip
We cannot slip
On something that's behind

RELEASE
Let it go

To find some peace of mind

Plastic Earth

Scattered plastic bottles
Fill our lands with debris
Ghosts from the consumption
Haunt our sacred Earth

I won't lose my bottle
Won't lie unused and empty
I'll fight for future children
It's what this world is worth

My Body Is A Temple

My body is a temple
Art strewn across the floor
Dishevelled mosaics
Lay tarnished with dusk

Books lost to the darkness

My body is a temple
Pillar candles stand tall
Bringing light to murky chambers
Rooms like shrunken lungs
Breathe the air of day again

Onwards And Upwards

Tap In To Your Potential

Living in a world of safety nets
Society's got us caught
Tangled up in the mundane
And the laziness of thought

They're building walls and closing doors
Stocking 'happiness' on shelves
Everything's too easy
We're sedated by their spells

No creatures left to run from
We're just running from ourselves
So break the trance, climb, advance
To a place where your soul dwells

Tap in to your potential
Of never ending wells

Trails and Tales

Eyes opened
Minds floating
In a different way
Don't ignore glorious stories
Or they'll just skip away

Tales that could have been told
Have never grown old
Trails that could have been traced
Were never embraced

It's time to face the facts
Nothing ever happens
Unless you react

Raise your sails to be amazed
New encounters really matter
So stop being afraid

It only takes two letters
To a person passing by
How will your day transform?

With a simple smile and

"Hi"

The Future's Our Creation

Beyond the broken minds of men
Above the beast we call consumption
Consciousness can expand
To cure the mindlessness
And destruction

We must resurrect this Earth
Resonate with a higher vibration
Retake our sacred turf
And rethink the role of nations

Together we can change
To eclipse the corporations
Things cannot stay the same
The future's our creation

Sword In The Stone

A rock so unrelenting
Heavy egos fail to yield
Many trapped within a mind set
Rooted in their field

Force and bloodshed
Tried and tested
Much lost and many slain
By green eyed brutes
In darkened suits
Looking for more gain

The Earth is our ally
We must listen to the land
Don't force our hand on nature
But learn to understand
It's not what we have
That defines us
Greed doesn't truly pay
Give without expecting
Surrender to Earth's way >

Clasp the hilt gently
With joy deep within your soul
The world is sliding softly
Towards our intended goal
We are stewards for the people
With hearts full of empathy
Have faith in the Universe
And all its mystery

Unprecedented

History will remember thee
Inhale scale and grandeur
Each breath a mural
Expanding utopia

Rise sky higher
Yet liquid fire
Can't melt angelic tendencies

At ease with the easel
Art trickles
Carve marble
With hammers and sickles

From zero to Nero
A kingdom of expression
Look behind the façade

A new kind of reflection

Ancient Journey

On this ancient journey
We travel our own way
Paying homage to those
We've never known
In the tracks of yesterday

In every step a lesson
Every mile a new insight
May your heart leave an impression
As you blaze a trail of light

Let the road surprise you
It can teach you many things
Stride for wisdom, strive for wonder
Find out what your journey means

Fit Together

We may all be broken
A little broken from the start
But at least now
The pieces fit together
Better than they fall apart

Hath No Fear

Hath no fear of the dark
Seek the stillness
Quell the chatter

For many a thought will
Come and pass
Yet none will truly matter

Withered Wings

When a storm doth come
To knock you down
And wings lay withered
On the ground

Remember that your fate's
Not bound
And good times will come
Back around

All storms pass
To bluest skies
And like a Dragonfly
You'll rise

Why I Dance

I dance to climb
Beyond the edges of time
Beyond the walls of my mind
It helps me unwind

So I can float
Above the mazes of grey
Above the castings of clay
In my own little way
I can repaint the day

Obsidian Skies

RISE
Through obsidian skies
With a chest puffed in size
Upon the wings of the night

REALIZE
That fear can be shed
From realms in the head
Expel the dread

Take flight

Anew

Every day, a new lease of life
It's black and white
Do what you like

Not because it's fashionable
The passion pulls
To it you fall

Keys

Many keys dangle before us
Many pathways drawn in the sand
Tangled stories, different doorways
All around us

New adventures
Waiting to be found

The Explorer

I am the explorer
Adorned in seaweed and moss
Shoes tossed off
I get lost in the sands of the forest

Warmed by the Sun
I trudge on to the song of birds
Looking for words...

Trying to find myself again

More Than You Think

Be sure of yourself!
Stand tall, don't shrink
Because it's highly likely
That you're made of more
Than you think

Get On With It

It might not come now
It may not be quick
So think about how
And get on with it

Because doing nothing
With our time
Is the only real risk

And a goal without a plan
Is just a wish

The Beginning Of Becoming

Lungs burning
In the cold air
After working
Beyond their capacity

Each breath spins dizzily
Basking in a warm glow
Of satisfaction

Knowing that you've
Given your all

When vision
Becomes action

Flames In My Eyes

I am the crackle
A white whip
From the Sky

I am the spark
To fire that flies

Charged by the air's
Deafening cries

Born from a storm
With flames in my eyes

The Wild Ones

Tooth and claw
The wild runners
Raving about this world
And there's others

Moving towards a goal
To discover
Paving a way
To the soul
To uncover
The raven inside
Of us all
Let's hover

Invisible Chains

There are no blocks
No blocks in place
No locks, no ties
No bars, no brace

We are shackled to shadows
Invisible chains around our wrists

They are not real
They don't exist

Sails

It's quite easy to drop sails
When life trails off course, it is
It's all about using resourcefulness

Instead of sleeping in the cabin
Waiting for something to happen
Start making it happen

Remember who's captain!

The Voyage

Crossing crystal seas
In boats of our own making
The voyage may be long
But the lands we seek are there

Diamond coated dreams
Act as our propeller
Spirits must stay strong
To take us anywhere

Journey On

Come rain or shine or brutish storm
Define your quest and journey on
Through the cold calm dusk
To the light lush dawn
Align your mind and journey on
Pass each test, you can perform
Find your best
And journey on

I Am Not My Past

I am not my past, for that has gone
The last mistake can't make me numb

I won't look at how far there is to go
But at how far I've already come

It's about what I do and the path I take
Not the things that I have done

It doesn't matter win or lose
I choose what I become

Moment Makers

We are the
Moment makers
The thrill chasers
Standing up to life's
Daily dangers

The game changers
Cosmic shakers
Rolling the dice
We are the
High end stakers

Living life
A little dangerous
We won't let anyone
Dictate to us
Drop the stress
Avoid the fuss
Life is too short then
We turn to dust

Awe

and

Wonder

Bow Before Yourself

Bow before yourself in awe
Embracing all your flaws and imperfections

Within us all is an indescribable beauty
A fortifying strength, an unstoppable will

Life is a miracle; a privilege denied to many
Seize the day, because in your own way
You are magnificent

Tamed By Beauty

Tamed by beauty, all darkness slain
Each close breath, each wistful kiss
And wishful whisper
Dissolves the chaos
Burning in my soul

As our bodies tied together
For a moment
The world felt no pain

The Gateway

Within the gateway of her eyes
Untold stories flowed
Raging rivers tamed
As images unfold

In her eyes I'm saved
My problems have been solved
I was lost, my thoughts had strayed
Now my fear has been dissolved

Isle Of Wonder

She is an isle of wonder
Shrouded in mystery
Longingly
I wish
To explore her shores
And belong
To part of her history

Other Minds

Do you often wonder
About the workings
Of another mind?

Stop to ponder
What's going on
On the inside?

Wishing to climb
Into their mind
What would you find?

Sulis

I sense your presence
Heaven sent a disguise
You are the mist
That lifts to the skies

I close my eyes
And welcome love in
You're the dusk and the dawn
Of where I begin

Each morning, heart soaring
Send a prayer on a wing
Let every word that I speak
Song that I sing
Be strong, be wise
Be pure, be true
You are everything and anything
All I have unto you

Where The Willows Sleep

Yonder, where the willows sleep
And hills are cloaked in green
I found a place of inner grace
I tapped into a stream

The source it coursed through sunlit pores
An ebbing, pulsing, flow
A force inside, a turning tide
I'll never let it go

Staggering

Everywhere I look is a perfect painting
New versions immerging
From years of changing

The ancient was patient
Whist re-arranging

Nature is staggering
And truly amazing

The Coming Of The Fox

In the silence of the bristling Sun
That brushed across my eyes
I saw in all her glory, a foxy figure rise
Fur glistening in the daylight
Flames lingering in her eyes
She brought me fire, took me higher
To a world where new words rise

When The World Begins Again

Listen to the breeze
Notice studded stars sparkling
Across a sky of oceans

Breathe in the scenery

Watch the new day slide forth
Across the perfect horizon
When the world begins again

The Watchman

Enveloped by the black of night
The Full Moon a lonely watchman
He strides towards the temple of time

Tied to tides of silver
Skin dipped in ashen dust
His heathen heart skips with wanderlust
As he throws himself, baying
To the glory of the stones

His Pagan soul drips with gold
Forsaking everything else
He is a servant of the Universe

Windows Of A Dream

In the mirror
Catch a liquid look
Watch a life glide down the stream

To silence turn in careful thought
And grasp at many droplets caught
In the windows of a dream

Strangers Passing By

In between worlds
And words we walk
Just strangers passing by

Parting people
We don't talk
Just strangers passing by

Wanderlust

The dust can never settle
The tracks are aching for my tread
In a world of the unbelievable
Visuals spill into my head

Every corner has an offering
Every hilltop has a view
The world is waiting for my footprints
Time to wander somewhere new

All it takes is a decision
Freedom dizzy in my mind
I'll take the plunge
Because I crave more fun
Who knows what I might find

The Sun

Lammas

Lughnasa

Lost in love below a golden Sun
Run your hands through fields of fun
Finger tips will guide the way
Trace a trickled trail around bales of hay

Poetic thoughts sail in the summer breeze
Dream a sweet dream beneath the shade of trees
Bright light flickers scattered serenades
As the new age illuminates
Don't let old ways fade

The Gift Of Kindness

To give is to live, let life be received
Through all befall our loving action
And within each and every
Caring fraction, all can be achieved
Look beyond yourself, Believe!

Kindness is a currency
No greater wealth proclaimed
Untamed it runs like roaring rivers
Within itself it shall deliver
More joyous a gift than can named
Its banks can't be contained

Look deeper if you want to meet her
Try to see each scene re-framed
Reflecting on every connection
And questioning all the complexion
What does it really mean?

To see the Goddess at all
We must see her in everything

I see her in the flowering Sun

In the rock and in the plain

In the moonlight over glade and bower

I feel the unity of her power

Through her, poetry roams untamed

Watch The World Wake

A veil of cloud
Sweeps across the treescape
The Sun is loud
As fresh beams escape

Watch the world wake
When a new day breaks

Don't Neglect The Sunset

I can't neglect the sunset
I have to stare at her dazzling glare
And once our eyes have met
I won't look away until the day
Has fallen, firmly set

Painted by the Sun

The world's painted by a lush plush crimson
A vibrant orange flutters around my vision
Sunspots connecting dots that live on
Pictures engrained in the back of the brain
Somewhere, someone, sits down, under the Sun
Playing their drum, letting their rhythm run
On and on until another dawn comes

Sun Chase

The Sun is mellow
Scattering yellow shadows
Across the freshly turned soil

Its beams mix with green tufts
Grass lighting a path alongside
Cracks in the raised mud

A trail of worn faces is chasing me

I look back to see the sunset
Breath through gaps in the hedgerow

Clouds relax in the distance

Wave Of Warmness

A gentle kiss from the morning Sun
Clung to the tips of their tongues
A wave of warmness sorely missed
Let them know that the day had begun

Autumn

Equinox

Mabon

Her Highness Lady Modron
Glides on beams above the shrubs
She drapes her harvest dress
To bless each gift with autumn love

Red and yellow hues infuse
The colours of her gown
Her garments glisten golden
Crimson, orange, auburn, brown

She bounds across the canopy
With a lightness in her feet
Dislodging fruits with tactile toes
So reap those treats and eat

Let's celebrate bountiful abundance
Because the light is fading fast
The last castings of the evening Sun
Show us summer time has passed >

Underneath a leafy roof
Let's drink the midnight air
For those who seek to find the truth
Just close your eyes and stare

Stare across an endless sea
Drop deep into your soul
Everything is energy
Unified and whole

Autumnal

She wants to stay
But can't get away
From Autumn's golden pull
She tries to last
And slip from his grasp
But she knows where this goes
She will fall

Fall for his charms
Fall into his arms...

Then all, will be autumnal

Lazy Evening

It was a lazy feeling evening
Sun lagging, light lying lightly
On everything

Warmth still glistening

Loose and easy
Flowers sit neatly
In the dreamy scenery
As a yellow haze gently
Sweeps the day away

Autumn Evening

The last glimmers of daylight
Can be seen glinting through the bracken
An orange glow emanates over the hedgerows
As lofty clouds slope towards the sunset
Amber rays dance over the canal
Its waters drifting towards nightfall

Energy Rushes

Splashes of sunlight
Spill through the greenery

A wild September warmth
Paints a pink haze
Over the horizon

All around an artscape
Crafted by brushes

Tonight's colours
Cover the forest with love
As a world full of energy

Rushes

The Way That It Feels

Two sides inside
Below and above
One fuelled by fear
The other with love

Clearing our thoughts
Will light the right way
Love is our source
A force here to stay

Make space
For your stillness
See what it reveals...

You'll know the truth
By the way that it feels

As Above So Below

We must first change on a spiritual plane
What we nurture we will grow

Nourished by rain, warmed by flame
We will reap what we sow

Look in, look out
There can be no doubt

"As above, so below"

Samhain

Ancient Stones

Relics stand oblong
Beyond the sands of time
Giant gifts given great baptisms
Grand signs of the divine

Colossal – enormous – regimented – rigor mortis
Each hard cased, slow paced tortoise
Brought to us by a raucous
Rambling, travelling crowd
Beating drums, standing proud

Chalices supporting liquid pearls
Hurled from the Sky
Beautiful moulded boulders
Rigid rocking stoned orchids

Shadows chime silent lines onto the ground
Thousands have dined and danced
In festive romance
Chants from crested tribes with outside lives
Casting blasting roars of alive
Yet never lasting >

169

Another generation subsides and turns to dust
Embers can be stoked, new folks on the cusp
Meanings have been torn
Feelings have been lost
See forlorn ghosts flicker
Amidst the hazy mist at dusk

For we are truly blessed
To stand within the vicinity
May these knowing nodules rise
Towards the skies for infinity

Sands Of Time

I stand upon this hallowed turf
The latest man to try his hand on Earth
The greatest strand of an unbroken line
That stretches back across the hands of time

The sands of time will not reside
Where ever we are, let's join outside
To honour the souls of those who've died
Because the meaning of life is to be alive
Within our short time here, let's try to thrive
Your spirit is strong you can survive
And any wrongs done to you, let them slide

When the Samhain dusk begins to fall
When the veil is thin and the dead stand tall
A Dragon rises inside us all
In jubilation we obey its call

Costumes, parties, feasts and flames
This Pagan celebration forever engrained
Love ones lost can be found again
The deceased live on, when you utter their names

Falling Leaves

Are they called leaves because they leave a tree
To fall upon the ground

Leaving what they've known, where they've grown
And the branch to which they're bound

They let go to begin again
Spread their wings, enjoy the fall

Because life is brief, for the leaf
When surrendering to its call

Spell Of Leaves

Swept up in the spell of leaves
Finding beauty in decay

To fall is to be born again
Such is nature's way

Moonstone Stare

Tonight has got that feeling
Like a changing of the seasons

There's a different taste to the air

Life will turn to death
But there's always something left

As darkness meets us
With its Moonstone stare

The Labyrinth

I walked a labyrinth last night
Through a heavy webbed mist
Under orange Moon light

Dragon breath candles lit the way
I spiralled through a maze
As the Samhain drummers played

Under the trance of the pounding drums
I could feel another journey had just begun
A resounding feeling span through my loins
As the two side inside of me, finally joined

Dust To Dusk

The Sky's regalia
Spills towards tangerine seams

Where the world peels off
And the skin of day
Is lost like dust to the dusk

Winter

Solstice

Yule

The Sun will rise from darkened days
The light brigade has found new ways
To charge the silver night with fire
To barge the darkness down the mire

This frozen grip now starts to slip
As strands of night abandon ship
A dormant world begins to quell
As nature inches from its shell

Great mother bears a new Sun king
His powers grow and lead to spring
He brings the evergreen spark of hope
And thus from him, new life bespoke

O'beauty found in hardened ground
In frosted webs and echoed sound
Through bird song carried on the breeze
In winter winds that shake the trees

With rattles bound in naked hands:
BE GONE the lazy, BE GONE the bland >

Awakened souls find untold gold
May darker parts start to unfold

Within our hearts we look for change
There's parts in all to rearrange
The path we walk is never clear
Yet it's done us well to bring us here

Rebirth is gradual, it will take time
No need to rush, take a gentle climb
Life can be weary and take its toll
Working towards a greater goal

Don't fear the night, for it must exist
But embrace the light like a heavenly kiss
Find sheer delight in earthly things
In clear blue skies and swirling streams

The Sun stands still, ready to rise
And with it the fire within your eyes
You have power, you have might
With belief, you set the world alight

We all have dreams and so should try
To help the dreams of other fly
Yuletide is about sharing gifts
And giving fellow folks a lift

During these twelve festive nights
We celebrate our Pagan rites
Our rituals give our lives more meaning
They cleanse and mend and help with healing

And even when you're far from home
Thoughts will always wander back to stone
Where for 5 thousands years people have praised
The returning Sun and lighter days

Winter Solstice

In the depths of winter
Find eternal sunshine
Shackled minds unchained
For we are more than cellular
The solar children
With visions of change

Fizzing flares of forward thought
Excursions beyond the blinkers
A new reign, a new game
For unbridled thinkers

Spirits pirouette
Criss-cross and intersect
Coiled energy reverberates
As exorcised egos escape

Now love dictates
Revamps and sows
It seamlessly streams
And flawlessly flows
Dreamily feel this force as it grows

Into
Turning tides sliding sideways

As light comes to days
Let hungry minds graze

The Fire Of Daybreak

The indigo sky catapulted to gold
Stretching back behind the horizon

Orange beams glistened
Across artificial tracks
The cold melting like wax
Under the fire of daybreak

The Returning Of The Light

From the depths of midwinter
The Sun is born again
Our light no longer taken
The darkness now defends

New avenues awaken
Each day raised to extend
The nightly grasp is shaken
From its clutches we transcend

Yuletide

Twas a night during Yuletide
When up in the Sky
I saw a great bolt of lightning
As Thor flew on by

Cracker and Gnasher
Were leading the way
The air rumbled with thunder
As they pulled his sleigh

Winter Sun

Let's welcome back the winter Sun
A returning of the light
A phase where days are raised
To graze until the lands are ripe

And soon late afternoons will bloom...
Instead of looking like
The middle of the night

So sing when summoning our king
For a Solstice warm and bright

Smouldering

The light
Came back from the night's
Embrace

Traces of stardust
On his shoulders

Smouldering

Ready to burn again

Imbolc

Imbolc

After a long and lonesome winter
Where light had lost its way
Amidst the brittle, broken, bracken
Slackened leaves had gone astray

From the gated ground, devoid of sound
Where frozen flakes once lay
I saw a hand come from the land
I'm sure it's here to stay

The fingers turned to lush green shoots
The nails they bloomed to flower
A bridge was formed by raising roots
I revelled in its power

I walked across the living path
That arced above a stream
I studied all the natural craft
Amazed by what I'd seen >

As I approached the other side
I saw a maiden fair
She stood beside two oxen
With flame red coloured hair

I was drawn towards her aura
Her hands enticed me in
She wrapped her fingers around my face
I felt her love within

She then turned and climbed upon her ox
Wishing me a fond farewell
I was still dazzled by her looks
Enchanted by her smell

Then all around in sight and sound
The world began to shine
I'd met the Goddess of my dreams
Been kissed by the divine

First Light

Intentions are lit like lanterns
Dragons emitting their glow
The first light shone
Will go on and on

Forwards to warm woods we go

Blessings

We are moving forward from new beginnings
Crossing over into the world of the living

Rumours

There's a rumour stirring on the wind
Whispers in the rain
Word from the ground is going around
That the light is back again

Phoenix Rising

Flakes of ash flash
Through a worn out sky
As the old world falls
To the wayside

Sparks leave seeds
To bring something new

A Phoenix is rising

The Phoenix in you

Another Star Is Born

A stream cuts across frost
On a cold winter's morn
The ground glistens like diamonds
The night starts to warm

A breathless embrace, graces black space
As darkness is chased by the dawn

Another day on planet Earth
Another star is born

Lanterns

Find lights inside that shine!
We all have fireflies
And star filled heights to climb
Lanterns lit and flickering
As we wander through
The night

Looking for more reasons
But inside the lights we find
That we choose our own meaning
By how we spend our time

How we decorate our skies
Concentrate our eyes
And decide to live our lives

Spring
Equinox

Introducing Spring

Rainbow halos, already steady, raring to go
Revving, rearing, appearing to glow
Clouds clapping and cheering, let's start the show

Grey curtains are parting to a hearty symphony
This ladies and gentlemen
Is a story of staunch poetry
It's the narration of germination
A programme of pollination
An orchestral celebration
Featuring some of the nation's
Finest fledgling choirs
It's a star studded cast

Picture if you can, our stage;
A circular meadow
With a narrow meandering hedgerow
Curving and swerving down the middle
This thorny fortress
Had thwarted the fauna from warring >

201

One side lay shielded from the Sun
Darkness had won
The ground lay fallow and barren
Yet one morning not so long ago
A tree yielded its seeds to the breeze
Some were eaten, some weather beaten
Most doomed to fail
But one seed sailed over the divide
And nestled neatly and completely
On the other side
Destined to prevail

This seed grew without light
Transcending eternal night
Its white leaves glistened across the meadow
Over the hedgerow there was a crescendo
Of colour and glory
A vibrant, illuminating, perpetual spring
A sumptuous, voluptuous, magical scene
Yet, in the middle grew an ugly black shrub
A tainted stub, in need of love

Spirituality is all encompassing
Transcending day and night

Because in essence they are the same thing

Life is a balancing act
In this theatre you can experience everything

We are the masters of our ceremonies
The drivers of our dreams
We are the day and the night
The darkness and the light

The Equinox

The Equinox knocks
Rings, springs into our lives
Let blossom be my bride
In her I will confide

Beauty Breathes

Budding leaves
Beauty breathes
Best believe

Appease the unity
Diverse but one
In conscious fluidity

Unite

To reach the light
Strive to unite
The ice and flames of conflict

Both powerful
With different pulls
Combined they will omit

A balanced force
A sacred source
And all shall benefit

Your Light

Your Light
Is dancing over spaces
Stunning Sun embraces
Now the night is chasing...

Pure life
New avenues awaken
Dazed we are extending
Shadows will be shaking

In your Light

Songs Of Spring

Written on the wind
A thousand songs
Of spring

As the morning spins
The world begins
To sing

Uplifting

Stems sprouting
Emerging from the dark
For new outings

Ground's waking
Eyes begin to blink

Pulsating

Light's shifting
Giving the gift of spring

Uplifting

Beltane

Beltane

Growth, let fresh starts flower
Seal seeds in the roof of your mind
Grow great thought towers

Truth is found in wild signs
Ley lines find power
Love sunny days
In mystic ways
And soft rain showers
Rise with the birds and add to your hours
Wise are the words of the old world founders

For this is a time to re-establish purity
Relinquish sin to the realm of obscurity
Bathe in the light
Misbehave in the night
Fumble and rumble and roar with delight

Ritual leaps as embers creep
Twirl like ribbons in graceful sweeps
Dance in transition
Make it a mission >

213

Let inner fires get higher
And spark your ignition

Offer gifts to the Gods and the faeries
Feed the flames with juniper berries

Show care and love
Be at ease
For we are one with the world
May there be peace

Please

Beltane Blessings

The wheel of the year keeps turning
May your May be full of fun
Keep all your passions burning bright
And bathe in the beautiful Sun, the Sun
This magical month has sprung

Nature's Song

One day she woke
To hear a song
Drifting on the breeze
Her feet were light
Filled with delight
She glided through the trees
She needed to find
The music
And hear the sound
Once more
But the harder she looked
The longer it took
The search became
A bore
So she relaxed
The sound came back
She didn't know
What to do

Should she lie and listen?
Or
Start her search anew?

World Of Art

I step outside into a world of art
Into the wake of a peach sprayed sky
I met with the Sun as he sinks to set
With a golden wave goodbye

I bask in the flow of the afterglow
As silhouettes of birds fly by
Just another day in the countryside
Seen through the lens
Of a different eye

Goddess

I create a shrine for you
You're my divinity, I feel affinity
With every aspect of your being
Boundaries receding
Living breathing fascination
From magical feeling

I believe in this love I feel
All aspects real
The truth has eluded me
For some time
But soon you will be mine
I combine instinct and intuition
To find the fruition of your wisdom
Lyrical ingenuity
Pulsates through me
Unstoppable poet visions
Disperse cynicism

I am the word of my forefathers
Soul bearers seek me while I sleep
This promise you must keep
Reminisce and move on
You're never too far gone
To pull back and realise that fact;
That life is not material
It's internal, eternal
Spirituality... That's reality

Summer
Solstice

Living In The Rhythm

Brought up in the crowd
By the beat of the drum
Caught up in the sound

Living in the rhythm

Passion is loud
Let's welcome the Sun
We are Pagan and proud

Happy Solstice everyone

The Mighty Sun

Humbled by the mighty Sun
In every golden strand
That weaves through leaves
Of plants and trees
To illuminate our land

Nature's Eye

The Sun is born
The Sun will die
The Sun will come again
A connecting thread
Through natures eye
That makes the cycle spin

The Moon will reign
The skies again
The stars are glistening
A departing Sun
May not have won
But one day he will win

Sweet Spirit Springs

Beneath the starry skies awake
Moons gentle kiss across the lake
Velvet ripples transform souls
Awash with mirrored liquid folds

Each wave stirs kindred spirits forth
Light licking laps of lunar force
Reflective thoughts of sacred source
The ebb and flow of all outdoors

The sweetest dreams of fresh embrace
Secluded streams meet sacred space
Bask in the ore of luminous lust
This nightly guide keeps pace till dusk

Above the horizon slivers burst
Sister Sun shines shimmering verse
Glistening, dazzling rainbow gems
As daybreak leaps like sprouting stems

Flowering new start, life ignites

Embrace the blue face of daily delights

Memorised by gushing beams

Rolling hills yield perfect dreams

Solstice

We came from fire
A constant burning, surging energy
Never empty, flame of plenty

Beyond the memory of man
Its warmth courses through our lives
Like the bloodlines of kings
It brings
Swiftly flowing streams of light
Our sight our soul our source
One spark unchained
Leads to many flames
Rising torrents of unstoppable force

Light to all that have come
And all that will be
Of all that have seen
And all that will see
Kingdoms rise and fall before
This burning ball of power
Showering heat and glistening rays
Brings light to life

And life to days
Praise be the almighty
The one, the Sun
Ignite me

Beaming Miss Majesty
Queen of the Sky
A star lit guide
With a scarlet hide
Found inside
She shines worldwide
And on the Summer Solstice
This star's longest day
We thank her with our presence
And pray for her to stay
Undulating, scintillating, colossus
Empress of our cosmos
We share your gaze with the ancients
Your body does excite us

Praise be the almighty
The one, the Sun
Unite us

The End

>⋮<

Mark Westmore is a Pagan poet, the 16th Bard of Bath, and the poetic Bard of Avebury. He has been performing his works in celebration of the eight Pagan fire festivals for the last eight years, particularly enjoying observation of the Full Moon zeniths in Avebury Moon Cove.

Mark enjoys walking the beautiful countryside in South West England and drawing inspiration from the landscape. He has been posting his poetry online for five years. In this book he brings all his work together, in homage to the written word and its impact on his life.

The Dragonfly has special significance to him. This ancient creature is his power animal and totem, bringing inspiration, sharing profound moments with him throughout his spiritual journey, and acting as reminder to be thankful for life.

The poetry in this book is a celebration of life and nature. It's written to bring the reader into the present moment, and to help them to become more mindful of themselves, and the world around them.

the.wayahed@gmail.com
www.facebook.com/wayahed
www.instagram.com/the.wayahed
www.wayahed.com

Printed in Great Britain
by Amazon